Walt Disney

Drawn from Imagination

Walt Disney

Drawn from Imagination

by **Bill Scollon**

DISNEP PRESS
New York • Los Angeles

Contents

Walt Disney

Drawn from Imagination

CHAPTER 1
Century of Promise

Walt Disney was born in Chicago at the dawn of the twentieth century. The world he entered was very different than the one he would leave. It was a time before the computer, television, radio, and even the movie theater. Most homes didn't yet have electricity. City streets, crowded with horse-drawn wagons, were just beginning to see the arrival of noisy contraptions called automobiles. And entertainment, for those who could afford it, came in the form of circuses, plays, and vaudeville — variety shows starring comedians, musicians, dancers, and other performers.

Along with the turn of the century came a wave of popular optimism. New discoveries and breakthroughs in science and technology were occurring faster than ever; these were advancements that promised to make life easier and more enjoyable for everyone. There were even some people, like the Wright brothers, who believed they could build a flying machine! Anything seemed possible. The century ahead held great promise.

Into this world was born, on December 5, 1901, a person who would, as much as anyone, come to define and shape what would be known as the American Century: Walter Elias Disney.

CHAPTER 2

Rural Beginnings
1901–1911

Walt was the fourth child of Elias and Flora Disney. The Disneys were a hardworking, churchgoing family living in a hardscrabble section of Chicago. Elias worked as a carpenter and a home builder. He built several houses, including his own.

When Walt was two, the family grew again with the addition of the first girl, Ruth. By that time, Elias and Flora were growing weary of their Chicago home. The city had always been coarse, noisy, and dirty. But now, there were saloons in the neighborhood and the crime rate was going up. Elias and Flora became convinced that the kids would be better off somewhere safer and more wholesome. The older boys, Herbert and Ray, were in their early teens. Behind them came Roy, age ten, Walt, and the baby.

It took a couple of years, but Elias finally found the perfect place. His brother Robert owned farmland in Missouri, four hundred miles from Chicago. Elias went to check out the area. It was just what he was looking for—wide-open spaces, fresh air, and a chance to start over. He bought a small farm and returned to Chicago to pack up the house. The family was moving to Marceline, Missouri. Everyone was excited.

Marceline was a prosperous town of 4,500 people in 1906. New homes in picturesque neighborhoods were a sharp contrast to the gritty and crowded streets of Chicago. Marceline's main street was lined with a variety of shops and businesses. In the center of it all was a charming park with a bandstand. It was the ideal picture of a small American town. Walt was only four years old when he got off the train in Marceline, but it would be a day he would never forget.

The family's new home was about a mile from the town square. Walt was full of excitement as their carriage pulled up to the whitewashed farmhouse. It had a wide green lawn rimmed with weeping willow trees. Behind the house were a barn, a corral, and forty acres of farmland. Young Walt felt like he had arrived in paradise.

The family worked hard on the farm, tending to fruit orchards and fields of corn, sorghum, and wheat. Walt had chores, too, but he also had plenty of time for fun. The chickens, cows, horses, and pigs all became his friends. Sometimes Walt would ride on the back of a pig, a trip that would often end with Walt falling in a mud puddle!

Not far from the house was a large cottonwood tree. On hot summer days, Walt would daydream in the shade of its leaves. He liked to watch the birds, small animals, and insects going about their daily business. Sometimes he drew them. "I became interested in drawing almost as soon as I could hold a pencil," Walt would later recall.

One day, while babysitting his sister, Ruth, the siblings came across a barrel of tar. Walt had the idea of using the tar to paint pictures on the side of the house. Ruth thought it might not wash off, but her big brother told her not to worry. The two used pieces of wood like paintbrushes and decorated the house with zigzags and stick figures. Before long, a sinking feeling came over them as they realized the tar would not come off. Their parents were upset, but the drawings stayed on the house. In fact, they were still there when the farm was sold, years later.

From time to time, other family members would visit the farm. Walt especially looked forward to seeing his Aunt Margaret. Each time she came, she would bring him pencils, paper, and crayons, a new invention. Walt appreciated the gifts. Money was always tight in the Disney household. His father, who could be very strict, had no intention of spending his hard-earned dollars on idle pursuits like drawing. For years, Aunt Margaret kept Walt supplied with drawing materials, "but most of all with praise and encouragement," he would later say. "She believed I was destined to become an artist."

When Walt was just seven, his confidence got another boost. A retired doctor who lived nearby saw that Walt's talents were developing and asked him to sketch his prized stallion. The horse wouldn't hold still, but Walt did his best. Apparently, the doctor was pleased. "He paid me a quarter for it. It seemed like a great treasure at that moment — my first sale of a picture," said Walt.

While in Marceline, Walt had his first exposure to popular entertainment. He saw a touring show of *Peter Pan* that starred a famous stage actress of the time, Maude Adams. Young Walt Disney must have been impressed. Many years later, when the studio was working on Disney's own version of the story, he contacted Maude Adams and asked her to review the script.

About this time, silent movies came to Marceline. Early films were primitive by today's standards. They were only shown in black and white. Color wouldn't come along until decades later. And the films were silent. The only sound came from a live organist who played along with the film. Still, people loved the new form of entertainment. Walt, with his sister, Ruth, in tow, snuck off to the movie theater the first chance he could.

The admission charge must have seemed like a lot. A chocolate bar in those days cost just two cents, but movie tickets were a full nickel—*each*! The movie, a religious story about the life of Jesus, lasted longer than Walt expected. It was after dark by the time he and Ruth got back to the house. Flora and Elias had been worried, but were glad to see them home safe and sound.

Walt was creating memories that would stay with him forever. But his father was finding that running the farm was too much of a challenge for him. The truth was, Elias was not a very good farmer. He was slow to take advice from more experienced neighbors and made mistakes that ate up his profits. The older Disney boys, Herbert and Ray, helped their father as much as they could. Still, after only a few years, the farm was struggling. One day, following an argument over money, Herbert and Ray decided they had had enough. That night, the young men snuck out of the window and left home. Without their help, the farm had little chance of surviving.

The next winter found Elias in poor health. First he got typhoid fever, and later pneumonia. Roy, just sixteen at the time, couldn't possibly keep the farm going on

 FAST-FORWARD About forty years later, Walt built a barn on his property in Los Angeles to use as a workshop. It was an exact copy of the barn he remembered from the farm in Marceline.

his own. So, in November of 1910, the entire farm, including all the equipment and animals, was put up for auction. Walt was heartbroken to see his animal friends being sold. He and Roy wept as they watched their favorite colt being led away by strangers.

When the school year ended, the Disney family was off to Kansas City, where Elias would start over once again. They had been in Marceline only a few years but the experiences Walt had there would inspire him for the rest of his life.

CHAPTER 3
The Big City
1911–1917

Kansas City, with over eighty thousand residents, was very different from the village of Marceline. Trucks and automobiles filled the streets, hundreds of electric lights lit up theater marquees, and people seemed to always be in a hurry. Walt missed the farm, but he found the energy of the city exciting.

Elias, now in his fifties, knew he had to find less strenuous work. The farm had nearly done him in. He signed up to manage newspaper deliveries for a section of town. *The Kansas City Star* was delivered every morning, and the *Kansas City Journal* was an evening paper. Elias, Roy, Walt, and other neighborhood boys would cover the routes.

The work was demanding. The boys had to rise early to meet the truck and load their papers into pushcarts or onto their bikes. And they had to adhere to their father's strict standards. It wasn't okay to just toss the paper in the yard like most delivery boys. If you worked for Elias, each paper had to be folded neatly and placed on the porch under a brick. In rainy or snowy weather, the papers had to be tucked behind the storm door to protect them. "Many times I shoveled a path through snow or walked across a picket fence on drifts to make delivery from my little wagon," Walt would remember. He wasn't exaggerating. Walt's first winter in Kansas City was the snowiest in the city's history.

Over sixty-seven inches of snow fell, a record that still stands today!

Elias paid the other delivery boys, but he kept the money his sons earned. "Your pay is the board and room that I provide for you," he told them. To earn some pocket cash, Walt secretly found other work he could fit into his schedule. He sold newspapers on the street corner, made deliveries for a local pharmacy, and, for a while, worked a few hours a week in a candy store. "It was tough going, but I liked it. I was earning money," Walt recalled. "Soon, maybe, I'd go to an art school to improve my drawing."

Walt held the paper route for six years, and rarely took a break. The job left him little time for recreation like playing baseball, hanging out with his friends, or going to Fairmont Park, an amusement park that was just a few blocks from his home. Still, Walt did manage to squeeze in some fun, often in the form of pranks. On one occasion, he

 CLOSE-UP What was a typical day like for Walt when he was nine? His day began before dawn. He got up at 3:30 A.M. to go and meet the newspaper truck. After loading papers into his pushcart, Walt would make his deliveries, getting back home by 6:00 A.M. Often Walt would take a short nap before having breakfast and heading off to Benton Grammar School. Each day, Walt left school a half hour early so he could pick up the evening papers. After making the deliveries, he would head home for a late supper. Then he did his homework and, usually, found some time to draw. At 9:00 P.M., Walt was off to bed. Tomorrow would come early.

dressed up in a wig and one of his mother's dresses, went outside, and knocked on the front door. His mother answered and had a conversation with the strange woman for several minutes before realizing it was Walt! When she finally recognized her son, Flora howled with laughter.

Walt attended Benton Grammar School. He was not a great student. Teachers noted that his attention seemed to wander. Walt may not have been keen on classroom learning, but he liked checking books out of the library. He read books by great storytellers like Mark Twain, Robert Louis Stevenson, and Charles Dickens.

In class, Walt was popular and enjoyed entertaining the other kids. He would draw a sequence of figures in the margins of his notebook and flip the pages to create little animations. Other times he would draw a funny face on the blackboard while making up a story about the character. Walt's constant drawing earned him a reputation as an artist. His artwork was good for his age and before long teachers had him drawing posters for school events.

When Walt was in the fourth grade, he caused uproar when he brought a mouse, tied to a string, into the classroom. "I would let him rove about on his leash under the seats to get a laugh from the other kids," Walt said. "Until the teacher rather sharply disagreed with my sense of extracurricular activities and made me keep the little beastie at home."

Walt was "very lighthearted all the time," his brother Roy would later say. "Full of fun." But the mood in the Disney home was often gloomy, in large part due to their father's sullen personality. Walt's best friend, Walt Pfeiffer, had a very different kind of family life. The Pfeiffers loved playing music, singing, telling jokes, and generally having a good time. They were so much fun that Walt was soon spending more time at the Pfeiffer house than his own.

The two Walts went to movies and vaudeville shows whenever they could. They liked to study the comedy acts and learn jokes. Walt and Walt began performing together, at first only for family and friends, and then in talent contests. Walt loved imitating the famous film comedian Charlie Chaplin and was, by all accounts, pretty good at it. Entering a talent contest as "Charlie Chaplin and the Count," the two friends won fourth place and split a prize of twenty-five cents.

When Walt was twelve, he went to school on Abraham Lincoln's birthday in a homemade Lincoln costume. To his teacher's astonishment, Walt recited the Gettysburg Address perfectly. The teacher was impressed. "My fellow pupils, too, seemed impressed," Walt recollected. "The actor in me stirred mightily."

Though Walt's job, schoolwork, and performing kept him busy, he practiced drawing whenever he could. He developed an interest in editorial cartoons. Sometimes he would go with his father to the offices of the *Kansas City Star*. "I was permitted to go into the art department and the engraving room of the paper and learn how things were done," Walt would say. It was becoming clear to him that he wanted to have a career in

FAST-FORWARD Walt was a great admirer of Abraham Lincoln's. He later created a robotic version of the great president for the 1964—65 New York World's Fair. The figure was surprisingly lifelike. Audiences often gasped when the mechanical Lincoln stood up and gave a speech.

entertainment. "Actor or artist—that was the conflict. Both goals seemed alluring."

When Walt's older brother Roy graduated from high school, he moved out of the house. He, too, had his problems with Elias. "He treats me like a boy," Roy said. He went off to work on a farm for a while, and then later took a job as a bank teller. Walt was upset. Though they were eight years apart and had very different personalities, Walt and Roy were quite fond of each other.

By 1917, it became clear to Elias that the newspaper delivery business was never going to bring him the kind of success he wanted. Ready to move on, Elias learned of an opportunity to invest in a Chicago company that made fruit jelly. He took all the money he had and invested it in the business. He also took a job there as the head of construction and maintenance. When Walt graduated grammar school, Elias moved the family back to the city they had left over ten years before.

Walt, however, stayed behind in Kansas City for the summer. He lived with his brother Herbert who, along with his wife and child, had moved into the family home when Elias, Flora, and Ruth left. Walt took a seasonal job with the railroad. All summer long, he rode the trains, selling cold drinks, candies, and newspapers to the passengers. He loved seeing the countryside and visiting other cities and towns along the way. Out from under his father's supervision, Walt was becoming independent.

CHAPTER 4

Growing Up
1917–1919

Walt was sorry to see his summer of riding the rails end, but in the fall of 1917 he went to Chicago to start high school. The school newspaper, the *Voice*, in an article about incoming students, noted that Walt "displayed unusual artistic talent and has become a *Voice* cartoonist." For the first time, Walt would have his editorial cartoons published.

By this time, World War I had been raging in Europe for more than three years. The United States, which had recently entered the war, was now sending soldiers overseas. Most of Walt's cartoons were about supporting the war effort and encouraging enlistment. Walt spent hours working on his drawings. After school, he also attended the Chicago Institute of Art. Elias didn't understand his son's fascination with art, but he did help pay for the classes. Walt had persuaded him that they were educational and not just for fun.

Walt also started writing down jokes and saving them for future use. He'd go to vaudeville shows and fill notebook pages with gags he thought would work in his cartoons. Walt would continue the practice of collecting humor for years. By 1940, he had amassed over one and a half million jokes!

The next summer, Walt and a friend applied for jobs at the post office. Though he was only sixteen, Walt drew a few lines on his face, put on one of his dad's suits, and convinced the employment office that he was eighteen. Walt worked long hours, but he was now making enough money to be able to take girls to the movies or vaudeville shows. He even bought himself a movie camera. Walt filmed himself doing his Charlie Chaplin impersonation so he could study his performance and look for ways to improve it.

As summer wore on, Walt grew restless. Roy had joined the navy and Walt wanted to follow in his footsteps. But that wasn't possible since Walt was too young to enlist. A friend told him that the American Ambulance Corps, part of the Red Cross, required their drivers to be only seventeen. That was still a year older than he and his friend were, but they faked their applications and were accepted. However, Walt also needed to persuade his parents to sign for his passport. Elias refused, but Flora, fearing Walt would just run away, signed for both of them.

As Walt prepared to go to Europe, he came down with the flu, which was devastating Chicago at the time. The illness delayed him for several weeks. When he was at last ready to ship out, World War I had come to an end. Walt assumed he would have to stay home. But to his surprise, drivers were needed in the post-war effort and he was sent overseas anyway.

Walt arrived in France just days before his seventeenth birthday and spent the next year driving relief trucks, cars, and ambulances around Paris. The city and surrounding area impressed him, and Walt was known to be a good tour guide for military officers. Of course, all during this time, he kept drawing. Walt's ambulance was covered in cartoons. He sketched Parisian street scenes and he sent political cartoons home to the high school newspaper. When the time came to return to America, a dock strike delayed the boat home. Walt and the friends he had made in the Corps spent three weeks relaxing on the French Riviera and having a ball.

Walt got off the transport ship in New York and explored the nation's largest city for days. He visited landmarks and caught up on the two latest Chaplin films. It's likely he also saw a new cartoon released that year featuring Felix the Cat, the first popular animated character.

NEWSWORTHY In 1918, the first airmail service began between New York and Washington, D.C. And a new appliance was finding its way into homes—the pop-up toaster. Too bad that sliced bread wouldn't come along for another ten years!

When Walt finally arrived back home in Chicago, his parents couldn't get over how he had changed. Walt had left as a boy and returned a man. And he had made some decisions about the direction his life would take. He told his parents he was not returning to high school. Elias hoped that Walt would want to work with him at the jelly factory, but the young man had other plans. He was going to Kansas City to be a newspaper cartoonist. It was the place he knew best, and not coincidentally, his brother Roy had already resettled there after his time in the navy.

Walt and Roy had a happy reunion when Walt arrived in Kansas City. Walt again stayed with his brother Herbert and his family in the old family home. Roy was living there, too. He was back to working at the bank and was dating a girl named Edna, who would later be his wife.

Walt was brimming with confidence and optimism. He gathered samples of his art and wasted no time in going to the offices of the *Kansas City Star*. Unfortunately, there were no openings for a cartoonist. Walt asked if he could start as an apprentice

 CLOSE-UP Later in his life, Walt would say, "My father never understood me. He thought I was the black sheep. This nonsense of drawing pictures. But my big brother would say, 'Kid, go ahead!' He said, 'Kid, I'm for you!' He encouraged me."

and work his way up. But the paper didn't need an apprentice. Because of Walt's experience in the Ambulance Corps, the personnel office suggested he apply for a job in the transportation department. Walt was annoyed. "I want to be a cartoonist, not a driver!" he told them. Walt soon found that the other daily paper in town, the *Journal*, didn't need a cartoonist either, though they promised to keep him in mind. Walt was disappointed.

Roy wanted to help his brother. A coworker told him about an opening for an apprentice at a commercial art company. Walt immediately went to apply. He impressed the employer with his talent and enthusiasm. Walt was hired on the spot at a beginning salary of fifty dollars a month. It wasn't a lot, but Walt would later tell his brother he would've accepted half that much.

Walt threw all his talent and energy into his first job as an artist. He was creating advertising illustrations for newspapers, posters, letterheads, catalogs, and flyers. The extra effort he put in, adding flourishes and original touches to his work, pleased his boss.

A young artist with the unusual name of Ub Iwerks had been hired just weeks before Walt started, and the two quickly became friends. They worked together on a number of projects. Unfortunately, the work dropped off at the end of the holiday season and Walt and Ub were let go. The friends tried starting their own business, but it was tougher to attract customers than they'd expected. A month later, Walt and Ub saw a job advertised for a cartoon artist at the

Kansas City Slide Company. The partners agreed that Walt should try and get the job, which they hoped would be part-time. That would allow Walt time to work with Ub, too. The head of the company really liked Walt's cartoons and hired him to work full-time for forty dollars a week. The opportunity was too good to pass up.

Within a couple of months, Walt had managed to get Ub hired as well. The company changed its name to the Kansas City Film Ad Company to keep up with the times. They were moving into short, animated commercials that would play in movie theaters. The short black-and-white silent films were popular with the moviegoing audience. Working on the ads was Walt's first experience with film animation, and he was completely captivated. In fact, he'd been on the job only a few weeks when he got a call from the *Kansas City Journal*. A cartoonist job had finally opened up and they asked

Walt if he wanted it. It's fun to try to imagine what was going through Walt's mind as he considered their offer. If he had said yes, his life would likely have been very different. But he turned the job down and the path for his future was set.

CHAPTER 5
Launching a Career
1920–1923

It was the beginning of the Roaring Twenties and excitement was in the air. The Great War was over, women had finally won the right to vote, and for the first time more people lived in cities than on farms. An energetic new style of music called jazz was sweeping the nation. And scientists were predicting that it would soon be possible to send music through the air so that people could listen to it at home. It would be called radio!

In Kansas City, the young Walt Disney and his coworkers at Film Ad were working to advance the art of animation. Walt wanted to learn everything about it. This natural curiosity was a characteristic he would exhibit throughout his life. Walt made friends with the cameraman and saw how stop-motion photography — exposing one frame of motion picture film at a time — created the illusion of movement when the film was projected. Walt also borrowed books on human and animal motion from the library. He and Ub studied the books carefully. Everything they learned, they applied to their work. Walt went further, rewriting some of the scripts, improving on the story elements, and adding jokes. The quality of the finished cartoons got better and better.

When the Film Ad Company began making short live-action films, Walt got involved in those as well. Sometimes he acted in them, taking roles such as a salesman or garage mechanic, and sometimes he directed the action. But animation continued to be his focus. Walt convinced the owner of Film Ad to allow him to take the animation camera home on the weekends. Working in the garage, Walt experimented with lighting, exposure times, and animation techniques late into the night. He was always pushing for improvements.

CLOSE-UP In 1920, Roy Disney was diagnosed with tuberculosis and sent to a veteran's hospital in Santa Fe, New Mexico. After a couple of years there, he was moved to a hospital in Los Angeles. Walt was sorry to see his brother go, and so was Edna. She and Roy had planned to marry that year.

It didn't take long before Walt started drawing his own animated shorts. He sold them to a local theater owner. Walt called the cartoons Laugh-O-grams, and audiences loved them. Walt's films gave him a small amount of fame and his confidence grew. He suggested to the owners of Film Ad that they move into producing regular cartoons, but they weren't interested. So, in 1922, Walt raised money from friends, family, and local businesses and started his own company, calling it Laugh-O-grams. He convinced Ub Iwerks to join him, then hired five more animators and office assistants.

Walt and his crew began work on a series of fairy tales. Their first cartoon attracted a New York–based distributor who ordered six new films. Walt and his staff were overjoyed. They started drawing the cartoons at a breakneck pace, sending out each one as soon as it was ready. Unfortunately, before Walt could collect his money, the distribution company went out of business. Suddenly, Laugh-O-grams was broke. The little company couldn't pay for supplies and couldn't keep up with the payroll. One by one, the staff had no choice but to leave.

Occasionally a small project would come in, but the jobs weren't enough to pull the company out of its slump. Walt, who by that time was living in a rooming house, began sleeping at the office to save money. Once a week, he'd go to the train station, where he could get a hot bath, complete with a bar of soap and a towel, for a dime. He ate on credit at the restaurant below his office. But he hit his limit when the tab reached sixty dollars.

QUICK TAKE One day, a dentist came in to the Laugh-O-grams office and offered Walt five hundred dollars to make an educational film on tooth decay. The result, *Tommy Tucker's Tooth*, briefly revitalized the business and showed that animation could be used to teach—a lesson that would be important to Walt years later.

Walt felt he needed to come up with something new to rekindle interest in his business. He had the idea of putting a live child actress in an animated cartoon and having characters interact with her. Walt sent off enthusiastic letters to distributors in New York announcing, "We have just discovered something new and clever in animated cartoons!" One distributor, M. J. Winkler, said she would be interested and Walt started production on *Alice's Wonderland*.

But Walt didn't have the money he needed to make the film. He did as much as he could, then wrote the distributor and told her there would be a slight delay. He then faced the fact that Laugh-O-grams was headed for bankruptcy. "It was the blackest time of my life," he would later say.

Although Walt was discouraged by the setback, he saw it as a chance to get into something new. He thought about moving to New York City, which was the center of the animation business at the time, to work on Felix the Cat cartoons. But "I finally came to a great decision," he would recall. "I had missed the boat. I had got in too late. Film cartooning had been going on for all of six or seven years."

Instead, Walt decided he would be a movie director. He had enjoyed directing the star of his Alice film and thought he could make a career of it. Roy, now in Los Angeles, encouraged Walt to come to California. To raise money for the train ticket, Walt shot movies of babies for new parents. In a few weeks, he had earned the money he needed.

In the summer of 1923, with forty dollars in his pocket, a half-full suitcase, and a sample film under his arm, Walt bought himself a first-class train ticket to Hollywood. His trademark enthusiasm and confidence were back. As he boarded the Santa Fe, California Limited, he felt "just free and happy."

CHAPTER 6
Hollywood
1923–1928

By 1923, movie studios had already established themselves in Hollywood, about ten miles from downtown Los Angeles. But Hollywood was sparsely populated at that time. Real estate developers were building new neighborhoods and competed with each other to draw potential home buyers to the area. One enterprising developer outdid the others by putting up a huge sign on the side of a mountain. The impressive sign, completed just weeks before Walt's arrival, drew curious visitors to the streets of Hollywood. With letters forty-five feet tall, and lit with flashing lights, the sign read HOLLYWOODLAND.

The train ride west gave Walt plenty of time to think about what might lie ahead. He planned to stay with his Uncle Robert, who had retired in Los Angeles, until he found a job. Walt was confident that wouldn't take him very long.

Over the next few weeks, Walt visited practically every major studio, introducing himself as a live-action film director. But with little experience to his credit, no one jumped to give the young Midwesterner his start. Walt offered to begin as an assistant director but still had no luck.

Roy suggested that Walt go back to cartooning. Walt resisted at first. He really wanted to be a director. But he came to realize that cartooning might be the only way for him to break into the movie business. "I was flat broke. I couldn't get a job," Walt later said. "Before I knew it, I had my animation board out."

Walt set up shop in his uncle's garage and began to draw again. He tried to revive a comic strip he'd been working on and made plans to animate short joke films, like those he had done in Kansas City. He also wrote again to M. J. Winkler, the distributor in New York who had expressed interest in the Alice film. Walt explained that he had relocated to Hollywood and sent her the half-finished film to preview.

CLOSE-UP A film distributor's job is to take a film, promote it, and make deals with exhibitors to show it in their theaters. The money earned is then shared with the filmmaker. A good distributor can turn an average movie into a moneymaker, and a great movie into a blockbuster.

In late October, Walt heard back from Winkler. She offered to pay for six films at $1,500 each and would probably want more.

Walt was overjoyed. He immediately went to see Roy, who was in the hospital recovering from a relapse of tuberculosis. It was late at night when Walt arrived. Visiting hours were over so Walt snuck into Roy's room and woke him up. "We're in! It's a deal!" he exclaimed. Roy read the telegram from Winkler and congratulated Walt. But Walt had something else on his mind. He knew he needed help making the films and running the business. He asked Roy to join him. Roy agreed and checked himself out of the hospital the next morning. That day, October 16, 1923, marks the official start of the Disney Company.

The Disney brothers delivered the first Alice comedy by December and soon had their first check. The brothers could now afford to move out of their uncle's garage and into a small office. They painted a sign on the door that read DISNEY BROS. STUDIO. As the workload grew, the studio added staff. Walt brought out several animators from Kansas

City, including Ub Iwerks, and hired assistants to ink and paint the animation drawings onto celluloid sheets. The cels, as they were called, were rectangles of clear plastic that were set over painted backgrounds. One of the people hired for ink and paint was Lillian Bounds, Walt's future wife.

Walt and Roy were surprised when they learned that M. J. Winkler had retired and her husband, Charles Mintz, would be taking over her business. But Mintz, who was also an experienced film distributor, was slower with payments, which left the fledgling studio in constant need of money. Still, the quality of the studio's work was improving and the Alice comedies were becoming popular. Mintz placed an order for eighteen more of the shorts, which helped put the studio on more solid ground. By this time, Walt was largely leaving the animation to his staff and concentrating on story and comedy.

With the business somewhat secure,

Roy's fiancée, Edna, moved to Los Angeles and the two were married on April 11, 1925. Just a few months later, on July 13, Walt and Lillian married. The brothers put even more pressure on themselves to make their business succeed. Anticipating growth, they put a deposit down on a vacant lot where they would build a larger studio.

It wasn't long, however, before the relationship with Mintz became strained. Checks were no longer coming in regularly and, to make matters worse, Mintz had cut back on what he was willing to pay for the films. It was the first of several hard lessons Walt would learn about the movie business. No matter how clever a film was, its success was at the mercy of distributors. They could make or break a film. Walt was able to come to an agreement with Mintz for a renewed contract, but by that time, it was becoming clear to everyone that the Alice films had about run their course.

The Disney Bros. Studio moved to their new headquarters on Hyperion Avenue (also in Los Angeles) in early 1926. They now had more space for the artists and room for expansion. The move was accompanied by a couple of other key changes. For one, Roy thought the company would sound better with a single name, so it became the Walt Disney Studio. The other change was that Walt had grown a mustache. He thought it made him look older than his twenty-four years—more suitable for a man with his own studio.

The next year, Mintz asked Walt to develop a cartoon rabbit that would star in a new series. Walt and Ub came up with a wacky character that Mintz named Oswald the Lucky Rabbit. However, the first test cartoons were disappointing. The character's personality was underdeveloped and the stories were weak. Walt and his staff worked hard to improve the cartoons.

They made Oswald younger, more appealing and put him in clever situations. In a short time, they got it right. Audiences responded well to the funny story lines and the more natural movement of the characters. Disney had to quickly add more animators—Mintz wanted a new Oswald cartoon every two weeks!

QUICK TAKE With the success of the Oswald cartoons, Walt and Roy could afford to build themselves identical houses on side-by-side lots less than a mile from the studio.

The contract for the first Oswald cartoons was set to expire in early 1928. Walt decided it would be a good idea to go to New York and meet with Mintz in person. Lillian would join Walt for the cross-country train trip. With the success the cartoons had been having, Walt was sure he would be able to get more money for the next films.

But Walt was in for a surprise. Mintz offered him *less* for each cartoon. And, if Walt refused, Mintz said he would hire Disney's animators and make the Oswald cartoons himself. In fact, Mintz revealed that most of them had already agreed. Walt couldn't believe it. He called Roy, who confirmed the news. To make matters worse, under the contract, Mintz was the one who owned the copyright for Oswald, not Disney.

The double-dealing angered Walt, and he was hurt to think his animators, whom he had trained and trusted, would abandon him. But he was not about to cave in to Mintz's demands. He stayed in New York for days to try and work out a new contract. But, in the end, Walt had to walk away from Charles Mintz and Oswald the Lucky Rabbit.

Through it all, Walt kept his positive outlook. He wasn't about to waste any time feeling sorry for himself. There was important work to do. As he and Lillian prepared to go home, he sent a telegram to Roy: DON'T WORRY EVERYTHING OK

WILL GIVE DETAILS WHEN ARRIVE—WALT.

Walt knew he needed a new character and began doodling in his sketch pad. At one point during the eighty-hour train ride back to Hollywood, Walt showed Lillian a little mouse character that he called Mortimer. Lillian thought the drawing was cute, but she didn't like the name. She said Mickey would be better. Walt resisted at first, then warmed to the idea. It was settled. The new character would be called Mickey Mouse.

FAST-FORWARD In later years, Walt liked to tell the story of a mouse that would visit his drawing board when he was getting started. "Perhaps it was the fond memory of him and of others of his clan who used to pick up lunch crumbs in our first cartoon studio . . . . that came to mind when we needed so desperately to find a new character to survive. Mickey Mouse's country forefathers, you might say."

CHAPTER 7
Mickey Mouse
1928–1932

Roy waited at the train station for Walt and Lillian to arrive. He couldn't wait to hear what kind of deal Walt had hammered out with Mintz. Roy was caught off guard when Walt smiled and explained that they had no deal. Instead, they would create their own character. After hearing the details of what had happened, Roy was fully on board.

Walt's return to the Hyperion studio

must have been awkward. Most of his animators were deserting him to work for Mintz, but they would still be at Disney for a couple of months. They had to finish the final Oswald cartoons to fulfill the old contract.

In his typical fashion, Walt didn't dwell on the setback, but instead got right to work. He moved Ub into a separate room, away from those he regarded as the disloyal animators, and the two of them began working on the new character. Ub refined the design of Mickey and helped develop his personality. Walt wanted his character to have the charm and humor of Charlie Chaplin. Mickey would be an innocent and friendly guy that sometimes got into trouble but always came up smiling.

Soon Ub was drawing the first Mickey Mouse cartoon. He worked behind closed doors at an incredible pace, making up to seven hundred drawings a day. A few trusted staff members did the ink and paint work in Walt's garage. Late at night, Walt would return to the studio to film the cartoon. Within weeks of returning from New York, Mickey's debut cartoon, *Plane Crazy*, was ready.

NEWSWORTHY In *Plane Crazy*, Mickey wants to be a pilot like Charles Lindbergh so he can win the heart of Minnie Mouse. In 1927, Lindbergh became the first person to fly solo across the Atlantic Ocean, making him a hero. A drawing of "Lindy" appears in the cartoon.

Walt previewed the cartoon for a small audience and was encouraged by the response. With the Mintz animators finally gone, Walt hired a new staff and got to work on *The Gallopin' Gaucho*, the second Mickey cartoon. But Walt was having problems finding a new distributor for the films. The best cartoon distributors were headquartered in New York and it was proving hard to get their attention. In the meantime, the studio began work on a third Mickey Mouse cartoon, *Steamboat Willie*.

The film industry in 1928 was going

through a lot of changes. The first film with sound appeared in late 1927. For audiences that had grown comfortable with silent films, it was quite a shock. Hearing silent film stars suddenly start talking was unsettling. Sometimes their voices weren't what the audience expected and many of them weren't able to make the switch to the "talkies." It's hard to imagine now, but many filmmakers thought that movies with sound might be a passing fad. Most animators agreed. They thought the addition of sound would destroy the effect they were creating.

But Walt could see that sound was the future of movies. Convinced he needed to do something special to attract attention to Mickey, Walt decided he would make *Steamboat Willie* the first cartoon with sound. Through trial and error, he and his staff invented a method of synchronizing moving pictures with a sound track. Walt then headed back to New York, where sound engineers and their recording equipment were centered.

Adding sound to *Steamboat Willie* took a lot more effort, and a lot more money, than Walt had expected. Still, he remained sure that this was his best shot at making Mickey a star. Back in California, Roy was having a hard time coming up with the money to cover the checks Walt was writing. But Walt wasn't discouraged. "Why should we let a few dollars jeopardize our chances?" he wrote to Roy. "I believe this is Old Man Opportunity rapping on our door. Let's don't let the jingle of a few pennies drown out his knock."

When the cartoon was ready, Walt screened it for several distributors. But they weren't sure audiences would like a cartoon with sound. To prove that they would, Walt paid for a special two-week preview of *Steamboat Willie* at New York's Colony Theater beginning on November 18, 1928. The cartoon was an instant success. Audiences fell in love with Mickey and were dazzled by the music, voices, and sound effects. The cartoon got great reviews in the press and people flocked to the theater.

Even then, distributors insisted on deals that would limit Walt's control. But he refused to compromise. Finally, an affable distributor named Pat Powers presented Walt with the kind of deal he wanted. It gave Walt more money and freedom than the others had offered. Under the new deal, Walt's studio began making one cartoon after the other and Mickey's popularity soared.

Walt was happy with the success Mickey was having, but he knew it was better not to rely on just one character. He came up with the idea for a series of cartoons that would run under the banner of the Silly Symphonies. Each cartoon would have unique characters and stand on its own. The first film in the series was *The Skeleton Dance*, which featured a graveyard full of dancing skeletons.

Once again, Walt had problems with

 QUICK TAKE Walt Disney performed the voice of Mickey Mouse until 1946.

his distributor. Money earned by the films was not being tracked properly. By the end of the year, Walt felt that Powers owed him a lot of money. But Powers refused to show Walt the accounting records. Instead, he offered to buy the studio and put Walt and his staff on salary. In fact, Powers revealed that he had already made a deal to hire Ub Iwerks to work for him. Walt took the news harder than he had when the other animators abandoned him. He and Ub had been friends since their first jobs in Kansas City.

 FAST-FORWARD The two friends eventually reunited and Ub returned to the studio in 1940.

Walt and Roy decided to break all ties with Pat Powers. Ub left the studio, and the Disney company was once again in need of a new distributor. But that would be easier now that Mickey was a star.

Meanwhile, Mickey's fame continued

to grow. The first products featuring his picture appeared in 1930. Also that year, an ambitious theater owner in Los Angeles started a Mickey Mouse Club. Kids would come to the theater for an afternoon of music, games, prizes, and Mickey Mouse cartoons. The idea caught fire, and before long there were over eight hundred clubs and one million members across the country!

Walt continued to make improvements in the cartoons. He and his animators were inventing modern animation techniques. Walt's drive to perfect the art of animation was relentless. He was also proving to be the kind of leader who could see the best potential in his employees and challenge them to achieve it. Background artist Peter Ellenshaw recalled, "He'd fill you with fire. I always tried to understand how he made me feel so good. It was magical, really. He said one time he was 'the bee that pollinated the flowers.'"

To improve story development, Walt came up with the idea of using storyboards. Up until this time, cartoons were described on paper and discussed at meetings. Sometimes, an artist would sketch out a key moment, but storyboards allowed the whole cartoon to be put in sequence with sketches of every scene. The drawings, pinned to a long piece of fiberboard, could easily be rearranged or replaced. Now everyone could see the story as it developed. Story men would present the boards to Walt and other staff. If Walt liked what he saw, he would often jump up and offer new ideas and suggestions. If he didn't like a story, he would sit quietly through an entire presentation. At the end, "one eyebrow would go up and he would start to cough or thump his hand on the arm of his chair," recalled a staff member. Before long, everyone knew that if Walt's eyebrow went up, he wasn't happy.

Walt used the Silly Symphonies series

 REWIND Walt's fourth-grade teacher told the class to draw a bouquet of flowers that sat on her desk. Walt drew the flowers with human faces and arms. *Flowers and Trees* took that moment of inspiration all the way to the Oscars!

as a place to test new ideas. In the early 1930s, a practical way to make color films had been developed, but it wasn't ready for live-action movies. However, the new process did work for animation. Walt made a two-year deal for the exclusive right to use this new method to make color cartoons. Roy Disney was nervous. Again his brother was taking a big risk and spending great sums of the company's money to do it. But he agreed to try it, and the result was the first cartoon in full color—*Flowers and Trees*. As Walt predicted, the film was a hit, winning Walt his first Academy Award.

CHAPTER 8
The Fairest of Them All
1933–1937

Walt Disney Productions, now with another distributor, was on a roll—but the country was not. It was the Great Depression, a time when the U.S. economy all but collapsed. Millions of people were put out of work as factories and businesses closed. Families lost their homes, their farms, and their savings. Across the nation, people lined up at soup kitchens and slept in shantytowns. In spite of these conditions, the movies continued to do well. The Depression-weary public needed a place where they could escape the grind of day-to-day life, if only for a little while.

In 1933, Disney released *Three Little Pigs*, the thirty-sixth cartoon in the Silly Symphonies series, and it was wildly successful. The Disney animators had filled every frame with personality and humor. The story of the three pigs being pursued by a big bad wolf struck a nerve with children and adults alike. The big bad wolf seemed to embody the fears everyone had about the Great Depression, while the industrious pigs were like average people struggling to get by. The cartoon's original song, "Who's Afraid of the Big Bad Wolf?", was popular, too. Disney had to scramble to start a music department as requests for song sheets and performance rights poured in. The success of the film was gratifying and firmly established Walt Disney Productions as the premier animation company. But Walt was already planning his next big thing.

As 1933 came to a close, Walt and Lillian, now living in a beautiful new home, welcomed their first child, Diane Marie, to

 QUICK TAKE Roy and other Disney executives urged Walt to put out more cartoons starring the three pigs. Walt reluctantly agreed, but the two follow-up films were not nearly as successful. After that, whenever someone suggested making a sequel, Walt would say, "You can't top pigs with pigs!"

the family. A second daughter, Sharon Mae, would come along three years later.

Walt had been thinking of moving beyond short cartoons for years. The constant pressure to put out one after another, in order to keep money coming in, was becoming exhausting. Walt believed that a full-length animated movie could be just as engaging as a live-action film, and he was ready to prove it. When Walt informed Roy that he planned to spend as much as half a million dollars to do a feature film, Roy tried to talk him out of it. But Walt had made up his mind.

CLOSE-UP The cost of a project never bothered Walt much: "All I know about money is that I have to have it to do things. Money does not excite me—ideas do."

One late afternoon, Walt told a group of about fifty animators to come back to the studio after dinner; he had something he wanted to tell them. When they returned, the animators sat on wooden chairs and

Walter Elias Disney was born at home in Chicago, Illinois, on December 5, 1901. He would play an important role in shaping the twentieth century.

Walt joined the American Ambulance Corps just as World War I was coming to a close. He arrived in France just before his seventeenth birthday and served for one year.

The Alice comedies (1924–1927) gave the Disney studio its start. Margie Gay was one of several actresses who played the little girl who entered a cartoon world.

Walt, on the far right, poses for a picture with his brother Roy, his parents, Flora and Elias, and his sister, Ruth. Not pictured are Walt's other siblings, Herbert and Ray.

From a very early age, Walt loved drawing. When he first moved to Hollywood, he tried to find work as a live-action film director, but it wasn't long before he was back at his drawing desk.

Audiences loved Mickey and his popularity skyrocketed. The studio moved quickly to extend that success to comics, toys, and other products.

Roy Disney was eight years older than Walt, and the siblings had very different personalities, but they shared a deep respect and love for each other.

In 1939, following the success of *Snow White*, the Academy of Motion Picture Arts and Sciences honored Walt Disney with a special Academy Award presented by child star Shirley Temple.

Walt could see an entire movie finished in his imagination and often acted it out for his writers and animators. Here, he's presenting a scene from *Pinocchio*.

Pinocchio was released in 1940 as the country was inching closer to entering World War II. The film was an artistic success, but ticket sales were disappointing.

One of the first employees hired by Disney Bros. Studio was Lillian Bounds. Walt and Lillian married on July 13, 1925, at her brother's home in Lewiston, Idaho.

Their daughters, Diane, left, and Sharon, right, flank Walt and Lillian. Though he spent a lot of time at the studio, Walt was a devoted family man.

In the late 1940s, Walt was preparing to enthusiastically lead his studio in a new direction. "Television is the coming thing," he told his staff.

Walt used his TV shows to build interest in the studio's latest movies, park rides, and, in this case, attractions for the 1964–65 New York World's Fair.

Walt had a lifelong love of trains. Park guests enjoyed seeing him conduct the train at Disneyland. Walt even installed a small steam train that circled his home.

Of all his many accomplishments, Walt had a special fondness for Disneyland. "It will continue to grow as long as there is imagination left in the world," he said.

watched as Walt, lit by a single light, told them the story of *Snow White and the Seven Dwarfs*. "He went through the whole story for us. From beginning to end, he performed all the characters and their voices, and we all fell for the story. We sat from eight until nearly midnight, spellbound," one animator remembered. It was classic Walt Disney storytelling. Walt saw the entire completed movie in his head before anyone had picked up a pencil. The job of the animators was to match his vision.

Producing a feature meant expanding the studio. Walt hired story men and sketch artists, putting them to work in an office next to his. The studio then began to aggressively recruit artists from all over the country, hiring hundreds of them. Studio facilities had to be expanded and new techniques were pioneered. To train all the new artists in the Disney style, art classes were held at the studio. Artists were encouraged to learn all they could about movement, expression, and action. They would go to the zoo, the park, or even the ballet. They even filmed certain actions in slow motion, like throwing a brick through a window. That way they could analyze, frame by frame, how the glass broke apart. Walt wasn't just training artists; he was building a community of creative people who shared his commitment to excellence. The employees had a strong loyalty to Walt and were motivated to go beyond his expectations.

REWIND Back when Walt was a fifteen-year-old newsboy in Kansas City, the newspaper rewarded all its carriers with a free showing of a live-action film version of *Snow White*. Thousands of kids crammed into the city convention center. The film was shown on four screens set around the vast hall. From where Walt sat, he could see two different screens. "The impression of the picture has stayed with me through the years," he would later write.

There were nearly five hundred employees at the studio by the time Walt was ready to begin animating *Snow White*.

They worked long hours under the constant pressure of making everything they did the best it could be. To relieve the stress, the animators enjoyed fooling around. They pulled pranks, played football in the hallways, and drew funny cartoons of each other.

As word spread about Walt's feature film project, his peers at other studios scoffed. They didn't think that audiences would sit still for a ninety-minute cartoon. It was sure to be a flop. Even if it succeeded, no one thought Disney would ever make his money back. Many began to refer to *Snow White* as "Disney's Folly."

It took over two years for Walt to get both the story and the designs for the characters the way he wanted them. Actual animation began in the middle of 1936, but filming wouldn't start until March of the next year—fewer than ten months from the scheduled premiere!

During this time, Walt and his camera

department invented a new way to film the animation. Called the multiplane camera, the device was a twelve-foot-high tower with a camera stand at the top. Below the camera were four different levels for the animation cels. Each cel could be moved separately from the others. By carefully manipulating the levels, characters seemed to move through scenes in three dimensions, creating the illusion of depth.

QUICK TAKE Many different names were considered for the Seven Dwarfs, including Scrappy, Cranky, Blabby, Jaunty, Dizzy, and Burpy! In the end, Walt settled on Happy, Sleepy, Sneezy, Grumpy, Dopey, Bashful, and Doc.

The invention was first used on a Silly Symphony cartoon entitled *The Old Mill*. The effect worked perfectly. Critics praised the film and the cartoon won Walt another Academy Award. With the multiplane camera, Walt now had the tools to make animation more lifelike. He was more convinced than ever that *Snow White* would be as good as, or better than, any live-action film.

The months leading up to the release of *Snow White* were frenetic. Scenes were being revised and redrawn even as the movie was being edited together. Walt was uncompromising, changing animation and story elements whenever they didn't live up to his standards. The cost of the film went higher and higher, costing over three times what Walt had estimated. The company had borrowed so much money that some feared the bank would take over the studio. For a time, there was a lot of concern that the film would have to be delayed. But through sheer determination and the combined efforts of hundreds of people working across three years—in the final months, they worked in eight- to-twelve-hour shifts, twenty-four hours a day—*Snow White and the Seven Dwarfs* premiered on December 21, 1937, in Hollywood.

It was a classic red-carpet event with searchlights tracing the sky and fans trying to catch a glimpse of the famous cartoon maker and the many movie stars in attendance. As Walt walked into the theater, he thought about all the people who said that no one would sit through a feature-length cartoon. Now was the moment of truth. As it turned out, the film captivated the audience from the start. They laughed, gasped, and cried in all the right places. When the movie came to an end, the audience jumped up and cheered. *Snow White* was a masterpiece, a triumph of filmmaking. Walt was delighted.

Critics and audiences alike loved the film. *Snow White* broke attendance records in theater after theater, and not just in the United States, but around the world. The movie quickly became the highest-grossing film up to that point, topping eight million dollars at the box office. That amount is even more impressive when you consider the average cost for a ticket at that time was twenty-three cents!

Songs from the movie played on the radio. And products featuring characters from the film were on store shelves. The studio was able to pay back everything it owed, and then watched as money continued to pour in. The success of *Snow White* made up for all the setbacks and dubious dealings that Walt and Roy had put up with over the years.

The movie's reception signaled something else, too. "We became aware that the days of the animated cartoon, as we had known it, were over," Walt would later say. Full-length animated movies were the future, and Walt was ready for it.

But coming world events would overwhelm his plans.

CHAPTER 9
Challenges
1938–1949

Walt Disney's fame grew with the success of *Snow White*. He received awards, honors, certificates, and a special Academy Award that had seven small Oscars surrounding a large one. Ten-year-old movie star Shirley Temple presented the award. Walt, who was never completely comfortable in the limelight, seemed to hesitate. "Don't be nervous, Mr. Disney," said the child actress.

With the long hours spent on *Snow White* behind him, Walt was grateful to have more time with his family. He was a devoted family man and loved to play with his daughters — chasing them around the house or splashing with them in the pool. One day, six-year-old Diane asked her father if he was Walt Disney. He laughed and said yes. Diane studied him and asked if he was "*the* Walt Disney." When he admitted that he was, she asked for an autograph.

The Hyperion studio had served the brothers well, but now that the company would be doing more feature-length films, it was clear they would need more space. Walt found the perfect spot in Burbank, just over the mountain from Hollywood, and the studio purchased fifty-one acres of land there in 1938.

As he did with his films, Walt poured himself into the design and planning of the new studio. It would be custom-made for animators with large art rooms, specialized furniture, and controlled lighting. Buildings were arranged to maximize the flow of work from animation, to ink and paint, to the camera department. Walt saw the studio as a creative community for artists. It would have the feel of a college campus, with plenty of green space and a snack shop. The new studio would be ready to move into by the end of 1939.

CLOSE-UP Walt and Roy moved their parents to Los Angeles in 1938. Flora passed away later that year. When construction on the new studio got under way, Walt asked his father, then eighty years old, to help supervise the carpentry. The work helped Elias cope with losing his wife. Elias died three years later.

While the new studio was being built, Walt put several new features into production. He became almost totally focused on feature films and spent less and less time on short cartoons. To handle working on more than one movie at a time, the studio added hundreds of new artists, animators, story men, and support staff, bringing the number of employees to over a thousand. And, as usual, Walt expected each new production to push the boundaries of animation in artistic merit, production technique, and sound design. That virtually assured that every new film would cost more to produce than the last.

The next two features to be released, *Pinocchio* and *Fantasia*, came out in 1940. Each one was wonderful, but neither generated the kind of revenue they needed to make them a financial success. In part that was because Disney had lost access to many of its foreign markets. The world was again at war, and its impact on the studio would be dramatic.

As the United States inched closer to entering World War II, the studio was again in financial distress. With the cost of building the new studio, the enormous payroll, and the losses from the last two films, the studio was in debt to the banks for millions of dollars. To raise money, Walt and Roy decided to sell stock in the company. The stock quickly sold out and the influx of money took the pressure off, at least for a while. Disney's latest feature film, *Dumbo*, which had been produced at a much lower cost, also helped by generating a profit at the box office.

The dramatic increase in the number of workers at Disney brought its own problems. Animators at other studios had been forming unions—organizations made up of workers that regulated working conditions and negotiated pay raises. Walt disliked unions. He wanted the studio to operate as it always had, with him overseeing a work environment that fostered creativity and commitment. But the studio had outgrown Walt's style of hands-on management. One of the employee complaints had to do with Walt's habit of randomly giving out bonuses to employees he felt performed above and beyond what was expected. As the organization grew, employees who didn't work under Walt's direct supervision felt overlooked. It was one of the things that led some employees to think they'd be better off having a union represent them.

Walt and Roy resisted unionization with all their might, but a group of studio workers pressed on. In the spring of 1941, Walt came to work one morning and found that a number of employees had gone on strike and were picketing in front of the studio. The strike caused a lot of heartache for those who had been with Walt a long time, and especially for Walt himself. He felt the studio system he had built was being destroyed. Negotiations took over three months, but finally the strike was settled. The animators joined the union and work resumed.

The United States entered World War II in December of 1941. The army immediately took over a large portion of e studio. Camouflage was draped across buildings, offices were commandeered as barracks, and antiaircraft guns were set up. An important airplane manufacturing plant was located nearby and the army was there to protect it from attack.

Walt wanted to help in the war effort and committed nearly all the studio's resources to projects for the government. His animation staff, depleted by nearly a third due to the military draft, created training and propaganda films, military insignias, and educational films on manufacturing, health, and safety topics. Walt also had the studio create cartoons to help keep up the public's morale, sell war bonds, and encourage people to pay their taxes on time.

In the meantime, only one feature film stayed in production, *Bambi*. With this film, Walt wanted to show that animation could realistically portray animals. The difficulty of animating fur and animal behavior, in

QUICK TAKE Walt later noted about *Bambi*, "One thing we positively learned is we need to never again spend so much time on a subject. We were nearly five years producing it. We made nearly four million drawings and actually used about four hundred thousand."

addition to constant revisions of the story, drove the cost of the film far over budget. To get the film out, compromises had to be made and *Bambi* was finally released in 1942 to lackluster reviews. It seemed that the serious tone of the film was out of step with an audience burdened by war.

When the war ended in 1945, Walt's studio was in disarray and needed to reinvent itself. The movie *Song of the South*, released in 1946, brought some much-needed critical and financial success. Building on the success of the nonfiction films the company had made during the war, Walt developed an interest in nature documentaries. That led to the creation of the True-Life Adventure series. The first film in the series, *Seal Island*, came out in 1948 and won an Academy Award for Best Documentary.

As the difficult decade came to a close, Walt had the studio positioned to again push the boundaries of popular entertainment in new and different ways. He would succeed, but not in the way anyone expected.

NEWSWORTHY A technology boom followed the end of World War II. Rockets were beginning to probe the upper atmosphere, the first electronic computer, which weighed thirty tons, came into being, and television was poised to upend the world of entertainment.

CHAPTER 10
The Small Screen
1950–1954

The 1950s were a time of prosperity for the country. Emerging from World War II as a superpower, the nation experienced a new wave of enthusiasm. Cheap gas and new super-highways meant families could vacation far from home. Commercial airlines traveled coast-to-coast in a matter of hours instead of days, bringing an end to the golden age of rail travel. And with wages going up, more money was being spent on entertainment.

Walt Disney was glad to put the last decade behind him. The war years had pushed the studio to the brink of bankruptcy. And several of the films released after the war, like *Make Mine Music*, *Melody Time*, and *So Dear to My Heart*, had produced disappointing box office returns.

Work had started on three new animated features in the late 1940s. Walt decided the first one to be released would be *Cinderella*. Because of cutbacks at the studio, a lot of compromises had been made in animating the film. Backgrounds were simplified, extra characters were eliminated, and animators had to cut corners wherever they could. There was concern that audiences would be put off by the shortcuts. But the concerns were swept aside when *Cinderella* became a huge success upon its release in early 1950. It was Disney's biggest hit since *Snow White*. The movie's music and merchandise tie-ins added to the revenue. The results lifted Walt's spirits and took the pressure off the studio.

The good news of 1950 continued with Disney's first all live-action film, *Treasure Island*. The movie, based on the classic Robert Louis Stevenson book, did well and proved that audiences would accept non-animated family films from Disney. Adding to that year's series of successes was the second True-Life Adventure film, *In Beaver Valley*. Things were definitely looking up!

QUICK TAKE The first television sets showed pictures only in black and white. Color TV wouldn't become widely available until the 1960s.

The big news in the entertainment world was all about the small screen—television. The widespread introduction of the amazing new technology had been postponed by the war. Now, TV was ready to take off. Although only 9 percent of homes had a TV in 1950, by the close of the decade, that number would jump to 87 percent!

Most film executives dismissed TV as nothing more than "radio with pictures." They were worried that if audiences could watch moving pictures at home, theater attendance would drop. But Walt didn't view television as a threat; he saw it as an opportunity. In 1947, he had traveled to New York—where TV networks were forming—with the express purpose of watching television day and night. He wanted to understand the new communications medium, how it worked and what was being shown. When he returned to the studio, Walt enthusiastically told his staff, "Television is the coming thing."

As 1950 came to a close, Walt aired his first TV program, a Christmas special for NBC, the National Broadcasting Company. The hour-long program featured Walt and celebrities "backstage" at the studio and showed clips from his next animated film,

Alice in Wonderland. The TV special attracted a huge audience, and capped a remarkable year for the company. Another Christmas special was planned for 1951.

The specials proved television's great potential to Walt. Television not only gave Disney a new outlet for his cartoons, it was also a great place to promote upcoming films. Walt was fascinated by the possibilities.

QUICK TAKE The first TV commercial aired in 1941, when TV was in its infancy. It was a twenty-second spot for a wristwatch. The cost for the ad? Nine dollars—about $150 in today's money.

For some time, Walt had been fascinated with something else, too. It was an idea that would take the company in a new and entirely unexpected direction. Walt wanted to build an amusement park.

At first, Roy Disney wasn't in favor of the idea. The cost would be enormous and Roy doubted banks would be willing to loan them all the money they'd need. After all, what did Disney know about running an amusement park? Walt understood that Roy was right, and he was in no mood to put the company's new financial security at risk. So, using his own money, Walt hired a few employees and set them up in a separate office to work with him on the project. As plans for the park grew more ambitious, so did the

NEWSWORTHY As Walt became more absorbed in planning his amusement park, he spent less time working on the studio's movies. Nonetheless, the animated film *Peter Pan* was a big hit in 1953. And, the next year, the company had another hit on its hands with the release of the live-action film, *20,000 Leagues Under the Sea*.

estimated cost to build it. As Roy warmed to the idea, he and Walt put together a financing plan that included limited investment from the studio, some bank loans, and smaller commitments from several companies who would have a presence in the park. But it wouldn't be enough. Walt needed a large investor to complete the plan. The answer came to him one sleepless night. "Television!" he announced to Roy the next day. "That's how we'll finance the park—television!"

Since the success of the holiday specials, the television networks had been after Disney to produce a weekly show for them. Enticing as the proposals were, the time just hadn't been right for Walt—until now. He would offer to create a weekly show in exchange for a large investment and loan guarantees for the amusement park. The TV show itself wouldn't make much money for the company, but it would be the perfect way to promote new films, merchandise, and, of course, the amusement park. Roy was supportive and set up appointments in New York. There were only three TV networks to choose from— NBC, CBS, and ABC.

But Walt didn't have anything for Roy to show them. All of his plans were spread across scattered drawings and models. Walt pulled an artist into the office one Saturday morning and worked with him through the weekend to create an aerial rendering of the proposed park. With the drawing and one page of notes, Roy took off for New York.

Both NBC and CBS wanted to work with Disney, but they had no interest in providing money for Walt's amusement park. It just didn't make sense to them. So Roy turned to ABC, the smallest network. Seeing an opportunity to boost the standing of the network, the company's president jumped at Roy's offer. In early 1954, the contracts were done, and in October Disney's TV show premiered on ABC. The program had the same name that the future amusement park would have—*Disneyland*.

CHAPTER 11
The Happiest Place on Earth
1955–1959

Walt had been thinking about having his own amusement park long before anyone knew it. His daughter Diane recalled that he would often take her and Sharon to small amusement parks and watch how people reacted to the rides. "He'd see families in the park and say, 'There's nothing for the parents to do. You've got to have a place where the whole family can have fun.'"

Often, when on a business trip, Walt would visit zoos, fairs, circuses, carnivals, and amusement parks. He studied what made them appealing, which attractions pleased people the most, and what the overall experience was. Many parks were dirty, littered, badly maintained, and full of unfriendly workers. Walt knew there had to be a better way.

Walt's lifelong love of trains contributed to his plans as well. In fact, when he and Lillian planned to build a new house in the late 1940s, the property had to be big enough for Walt to have his own train! He and his studio engineers built the train with careful attention to every detail and tested it at the studio. When it was ready, the train was installed on a half-mile track that ran around his property. Walt loved wearing his engineer's cap and giving his daughters or visitors a ride. When they got back to the house, it was time for an ice cream soda at Walt's own soda fountain.

As plans for the amusement park came together, a passenger train that ran around the park became a main feature. At first, Walt wanted to build the park right next to the studio in Burbank. It would be called Mickey Mouse Park. There would be a roller coaster, a merry-go-round, an old western town, and a section of carnival games. But the longer Walt worked on the idea, the more attractions he added. Before long, it became clear that the area near the studio wouldn't be big enough to hold all his ideas. Walt would have to find another location.

To develop the park, Walt formed a separate company using his initials for its name, WED Enterprises. Known now as Imagineering, WED was a small creative workshop where new ideas could be tried out away from the day-to-day pressures of running the studio.

The staff of WED was made up of talent Walt recruited from across the company.

There were artists, animators, designers, engineers, writers, filmmakers, model builders, and more. Everyone contributed to the development of every aspect of the park, which by then was called Disneyland. The different skills, talents, and points of view of the workers enriched each idea. Walt liked working at WED so much he called it his "sandbox."

By the time ABC came on board, 160 acres of orange groves had already been purchased in Anaheim, about forty miles south of the studio. Walt's vision for Disneyland was coming together. Where other amusement parks were chaotic and dirty, Disneyland would be carefully designed and spotless. The park would be steeped in American traditions, history, and experiences. Walt wanted kids and parents alike to come away having learned something new. The people who came to the park would be treated like guests, not customers, and employees would be called cast members. When cast members were in the park, they would be onstage and part of the show, the overall experience of Disneyland.

The layout for the park was a virtual map of Walt's imagination. A train station set upon a bluff marked the entrance to the park. Guests would first experience Main Street, USA—an idealized version of small towns like Marceline, Missouri, where Walt had lived as a small boy. The Sleeping Beauty castle, visible in the distance, would draw people to a central hub. From there, sidewalks, arranged like spokes on a wheel, would lead them to Adventureland, Frontierland, Fantasyland, and Tomorrowland.

QUICK TAKE During the park's development, plans were shown to a group of top amusement park operators to get their opinions. After reviewing the plans, the men agreed that Disneyland was a bad idea. They said there weren't enough rides, there was too much open space, and the complicated ride systems wouldn't work. They strongly advised Walt to abandon the project.

Building Disneyland was an enormous task. Walt had promised the park would open in the summer of 1955. By the time construction began, opening day was just eleven months away. Trees had to be cleared, rivers dug, water and sewer lines run, electricity brought in, and tons of concrete and asphalt had to be laid for streets, pathways, and building foundations. A grand castle, riverboat, and train had to be built. An entire street of shops and restaurants needed to go up. Rides were constructed and tested at the studio, then trucked to Anaheim. Walt was there constantly, personally overseeing all aspects of construction. He insisted on uncompromising attention to every detail, from the contours of the land to the buttons on each cast member's costume. "The thing that's going to make Disneyland unique and different is the detail," Walt explained. "If we lose the detail, we lose it all."

Naturally, with a construction project

that big, there were bound to be a number of setbacks. But no matter what, postponing opening day was not an option. The park was being promoted every week on the *Disneyland* TV show. Regular progress reports and looks behind the scenes were building up public excitement. The program was basically one long commercial for Disneyland and Disney films, but viewers loved it. It was one of the most entertaining shows on television.

CLOSE-UP During construction, Walt would often tell the engineers to crouch down next to him and imagine how a building would look from a low angle. He wanted them to appreciate how a child would experience the park.

The biggest hit to come out of the *Disneyland* TV show's first season was "Davy Crockett." The five-part miniseries about the famous frontiersman sparked a craze that swept the country. The program's theme song was at the top of the popular music charts for months. At the peak of Crockett's popularity, stores were selling five thousand coonskin caps, just like the one Davy wore, every day!

With most of the construction finished, Disneyland opened on July 17, 1955. It was an immediate success. A much larger crowd than had been expected streamed down Main Street. Ninety million viewers, who were watching it all live on TV, joined them.

Twenty attractions greeted guests to the new park, including the Jungle Cruise, the *Mark Twain Riverboat*, King Arthur Carrousel, Peter Pan's Flight, and Rocket to the Moon (which opened five days after the park's unveiling). Surrounding it all was the Disneyland Railroad.

The park had its share of opening day problems. The heat of the day softened the new asphalt on Main Street, causing shoes to stick. There weren't enough water fountains. And some of the rides stopped working. But in the days that followed, Walt and his team

NEWSWORTHY Walt dedicated his park with these words: "To all who come to this happy place, welcome. Disneyland is your land. Here age relives fond memories of the past, and here youth may savor the challenge and promise of the future. Disneyland is dedicated to the ideals, the dreams, and the hard facts that have created America . . . with the hope that it will be a source of joy and inspiration to all the world."

addressed every problem. In any event, the missteps didn't seem to keep anyone away. The park welcomed its one-millionth guest just seven weeks after opening day!

Meanwhile, the studio was turning out hit after hit, on TV and at theaters. *The Mickey Mouse Club*, a one-hour daily show, began airing in 1955. The program featured a live cast of kids, musical numbers, skits, cartoons, and short dramatic and nature segments. The show was immediately popular and routinely attracted nearly half of all TV viewers. In theaters that year, *Lady and the Tramp*, an animated feature, had a very successful run. Over the next years, the studio released numerous animated shorts, nature documentaries, and live-action movies, including *Old Yeller* and *Johnny Tremain*.

Unlike a movie or TV show that had to be finished and released at some point, Disneyland would keep changing, growing, and improving. Walt couldn't have been happier about that. "Disneyland will never be completed," he said. "It will continue to grow as long as there is imagination left in the world." In the park's second year, more than twelve new attractions were added, including the Rainbow Caverns Mine Train, Storybook Land, Tom Sawyer Island, and the Astro-Jets.

The studio's next animated movie to be released, *Sleeping Beauty*, was its most costly yet. But the artistic film, drawn in a style completely different from earlier Disney animated features, did not do well at the box office. As some of the film's animators had feared, the art lacked warmth and audience appeal. The film had also lacked Walt's attention due to the construction of the park. But with the ongoing success of other films, TV projects, Disneyland, music, and merchandise, the company was better able to absorb the losses. In fact, by the end of the

1950s, Disney was in better financial shape than it had ever been.

But Walt Disney wasn't about to slow down. He was quietly beginning work on a mysterious venture called "Project X."

CHAPTER 12
Looking East
1960–1965

Disneyland's unrivaled success and the studio's track record of producing hit after hit brought virtually universal acclaim to Walt Disney. He had received practically every award he could from the entertainment industry and his regular TV appearances made him one of the most famous people in the world. All this success meant his studio was making lots of money. "For the first time, the banks owe me money!" he joked to a reporter. Walt was ready for new challenges.

The 1960s brought social changes, scientific discoveries, and new inventions at breakneck speed. Rock and roll blared from transistor radios; powerful beams of light called lasers were devised; astronauts were shot into space; and computers became friendlier with the invention of the mouse. One development that was particularly interesting to Walt was color TV.

The deal with ABC had been good for Disney, but in recent years the network had put more restrictions on the kind of programs it would accept. After a lot of back and forth, Disney bought out ABC's stake in Disneyland and the two companies parted ways. Walt wanted his next TV deal to be with ABC's rival, NBC.

NBC was anxious to begin airing programs in color. Its parent company, RCA, was mass-producing color television sets and

needed to give people a reason to replace their black-and-white TVs.

Walt, who had pioneered color movies,

couldn't wait to make color TV shows, too. The deal, which put no restrictions on what Walt could produce, was quickly agreed to. In September of 1961, the first *Walt Disney's Wonderful World of Color* program went on the air and changed television history. The public loved the show and the sale of color TVs skyrocketed! It was another milestone for Walt and his company.

As Walt's sixtieth birthday approached, he began to think about what he wanted to be remembered for. He wanted to do something beyond entertainment, something that would make an impact on society. He wanted to start a school for the creative and performing arts.

Even before the days when Walt provided his animators with art classes at the studio, he'd had a deep appreciation for quality education. In 1961, with Walt's help and generosity, two small colleges in Los Angeles, an art school and a music school, agreed to join together and form the California Institute of the Arts (CalArts). Under Walt's guidance, CalArts would provide a new approach to arts education. All kinds of artists and performers would be taught at the same school. "It's the principle thing I hope to leave when I move on to greener pastures," he said. "If I can help provide a place to develop the talent of the future, I think I will have accomplished something." Today, CalArts has educated more than fifteen thousand students and is rated one of the top arts schools in the world.

Meanwhile, as Walt was working on putting CalArts together, the Disney studio continued its string of hit movies. Among them was *Swiss Family Robinson*, a live-action film about a family of castaways, which made ten times the amount of money it had cost to produce. The animated film *One Hundred and One Dalmatians* was also a remarkable success.

But the art of animation was changing

again, and many thought it was not for the better. Because of rising wages, the cost of inking character outlines by hand had become very expensive. The solution was to photocopy drawings directly onto cels instead of having them drawn by hand. The process was used for the first time on *101 Dalmatians*. Many felt the technique made the animation feel sketchier. But the moviegoing audience loved the film just the same.

Disneyland continued to add attractions and rides. Moreover, Walt and his team were creating four brand-new attractions for the 1964–1965 World's Fair in New York. There were two main reasons Walt wanted to work on the World's Fair. First, the fair would serve as a test site for new attractions, all of which would be paid for by private companies. The second reason was to see if Disney-style attractions would be as popular in the eastern part of the country as they were in the west. Walt was in the early stages of planning for a second Disneyland, but he needed to be sure it would be a success.

One of the projects being developed was especially near to Walt's heart. He was building a remarkably lifelike robot of President Lincoln that would stand up and deliver portions of his famous speeches. The technology had been in development for a while at WED, but making it reliable enough to work as an attraction—and realistic enough to please Walt—was a tremendous challenge. Because the system required the use of sound, animation, and electronics, it became known as Audio-Animatronics.

Disney engineers worked long hours to perfect the technology. Walt encouraged them to keep at it, saying, "If you can dream it, you can do it." Mr. Lincoln was at last installed at the New York fair just days before its first scheduled performance. Though the robot had worked beautifully in California, it didn't work in New York. Engineers thought

 REWIND Walt's daughter Diane remembered, "When we went to Paris, Dad went off on his own and came back with boxes and boxes of little windup toys. He said, 'Look at that movement, with just a simple mechanism.' He was studying; he could see Audio-Animatronics. We thought he was crazy."

perhaps the damp air had something to do with it. Or maybe it was the fair's electrical service. Whatever the reason, Mr. Lincoln simply would not work properly. As Walt watched, his technicians kept trying, right up until the curtain was to be raised. Walt went out front to talk to the audience. He smiled and said, "There isn't going to be any show." The audience thought he was kidding. "It's true. We've worked like beavers to get it ready, but it's not ready and I won't show it to you until it is. I'm sorry," he said. It took another week, but at last, Mr. Lincoln was working as planned.

Great Moments with Mr. Lincoln quickly became the most popular attraction at the fair, and Disney's unfortunate delay was all but forgotten.

The other Disney-made attractions at the fair were also popular. It's a Small World was a boat ride that took visitors through groupings of dolls dressed to represent children from all over the world. The simplified Audio-Animatronics figures sang a catchy theme song as guests floated by. The Carousel of Progress also featured

Audio-Animatronics. In this attraction about the growing importance of electricity through the years, the audience area rotated around a circular stage. The fourth Disney attraction was the Magic Skyway (for Ford), a ride that took visitors on a journey through time to dinosaurs, cavemen, and a fantastic city of tomorrow.

At the end of the fair's two-year run, the attractions were packed up and installed at Disneyland. Based on the response he had gotten, Walt knew that his plans for an eastern U.S. Disneyland would be a success.

NEWSWORTHY Another Disney movie struck gold in 1964—*Mary Poppins*. The live-action film, which includes animated segments, is one of Disney's best-loved pictures. In addition to taking in huge box-office receipts, *Mary Poppins* was nominated for an amazing thirteen Oscars, winning five.

In 1963, Walt pulled a trusted team of executives together and told them he wanted to begin buying up thousands of acres of land in central Florida—the location he had settled on for the second Disneyland. It had to be done in secret, however. If landowners found out that the buyer was Disney, property prices would shoot up. The secret had to be kept from coworkers, too. The Florida plan would have a code name—Project X.

By the middle of 1965, Walt's team had succeeded beyond expectations. They had purchased over forty-three square miles—an area twice the size of Manhattan Island—at bargain prices. Walt wanted to have control of all the land around his new park to avoid the unsightly hodgepodge of cheap motels and restaurants that sprang up after the original Disneyland opened.

But there was another reason Walt wanted such an expansive space. He was planning to build a city. He envisioned a place called EPCOT, which stands for the Experimental Prototype Community of Tomorrow. Walt hoped EPCOT would be a functioning city of over twenty thousand people. Some would work at the new park, and others in a downtown business district. Residents would live in apartments and homes arranged around the civic center. Below the city, there would be a system of roads and tunnels that would handle mass transportation, garbage collection, and water and electrical lines. EPCOT would be a showcase for new technologies, materials, and ideas. Walt wanted to show how the quality of life could be improved in urban areas. He imagined EPCOT to be "a community of tomorrow, that will never be completed." It was his most ambitious and daring plan yet.

In November of 1965, Project X was finally revealed to the world at a Florida press conference. It was announced that work on the new Disneyland would begin immediately. Walt was energized. There was much to do.

CHAPTER 13
Untimely Passing
1966

Walt began 1966 by serving as the Grand Marshal for the annual Tournament of Roses Parade in Pasadena, California. The year ahead would prove to be as busy as any year Walt had known.

At Disneyland, new attractions were opened, including the It's a Small World ride and a new themed area called New Orleans Square. The studio released several live-action films during the year, as well as the animated film *Winnie the Pooh and the Honey Tree*. Walt was again involving himself more deeply in film production. Two projects in particular were keeping him busy: the animated film *The Jungle Book* and a live-action film called *The Happiest Millionaire*. And he was continuing to appear weekly as the host of the *Walt Disney's Wonderful World of Color* TV show. On top of all that, every moment he could spare was given to developing the projects in Florida.

But those who worked most closely with Walt noticed that he had less energy and was becoming more irritable. An old injury to his neck was acting up, sending shooting pains down his back and into his legs. He had a chronic sinus condition and it was easy for him to catch a cold. Still, through it all, Walt continued to smoke cigarettes. It was a habit he had picked up while overseas nearly fifty years before.

In July, Walt took his entire family

on a vacation. By now, his daughters were both married and had given Walt and Lilly seven grandchildren. They went on a small cruise ship in Canada. But during this trip, it became obvious to his family that Walt wasn't feeling well. His mood was subdued and his voice was becoming raspier. Sometimes he seemed to have trouble getting on and off the boat.

After the vacation, Walt went right back to his busy schedule. But pain from the injury became too much. He entered the hospital in early November planning to have a routine procedure done to relieve the pain. But while he was there, an X-ray revealed that he had lung cancer. Doctors said they needed to remove one of his lungs. The surgery was successful, but the doctor had grim news. Walt's other lung was diseased as well. At best, he only had a couple of years left. The family was stunned. No one had suspected he was that sick.

 CLOSE-UP In the hospital, Walt told his son-in-law Ron Miller, "If I could live for fifteen more years, I would surpass everything I've done over the past forty years."

After two weeks in the hospital, Walt returned to work for a few days. But he was clearly seriously ill and he tired easily.

It wasn't long before Walt was back in the hospital. His condition seemed to improve slightly, raising the family's hopes. Roy visited his brother often. One night, Walt used the grid of ceiling tiles above his hospital bed as a map of the Florida property. He raised his hand and pointed out to Roy where roads, buildings, and attractions should go. The next day, December 15, 1966, Walt Disney passed away at the age of sixty-five.

Family, friends, employees, and people everywhere were shocked. The world had lost a creative genius, a brilliant innovator, and a master storyteller. There would never be another Walt Disney.

During his career, Walt Disney was presented with twenty-two Academy Awards, which, to this day, is far more than any other individual. For excellence in television production, Walt and his staff received seven Emmy Awards. He was also given hundreds of honors and commendations from universities, professional groups, and governments around the world. President Lyndon Johnson awarded Walt the Presidential Medal of Freedom, the country's highest civilian honor. But with all his accomplishments, fame, and success, Walt was uncomfortable with excessive praise. To keep things in perspective, he liked to say, "I only hope that we never lose sight of one thing: that it was all started by a mouse."

Roy Disney, who had been planning to retire, stayed on after his brother's death and completed the Florida theme park, which he named Walt Disney World. The park opened in October of 1971. Roy Disney died just two months later.

Since that time, The Walt Disney Company has grown considerably. Disney resorts and theme parks can be found around the world. Disney owns companies such as ABC, ESPN, Pixar, Lucasfilm, and Marvel. Disney is a world leader in every facet of entertainment: movies, television, stage shows, home entertainment, interactive games, Internet programming, music, books, magazines, products, and more.

With all that growth you might think the company has gone as far as it can. But you'd be wrong. As Walt Disney once told his staff, "I just want to leave you with this thought—that it's just been sort of a dress rehearsal and we're just getting started. So if any of you start resting on your laurels, I mean just forget it, because . . . we are just getting started."

Discussion Questions

1) What did you like most about the book? What new things did you learn?
2) Name a few of the people and places that influenced Walt. How did those people or places affect him?
3) Walt had several setbacks in his career. How did he deal with them? Give at least one example.

4) Walt Disney's life spanned a period of great social change and scientific progress. Name a few of the events and inventions that occurred during his lifetime.

5) What do you think were Walt Disney's greatest accomplishments and why? What did he want to be remembered for?

6) Walt Disney has been described as one of the world's greatest storytellers. Do you agree? Why or why not?

7) Did your opinion of Walt Disney change as a result of reading this book? If so, how?

8) Walt Disney said he wanted people to remember, "It was all started by a mouse." What do you think that means? Why did he think that was important?

Bibliography

Burnes, Brian, et al. *Walt Disney's Missouri: The Roots of a Creative Genius.* Kansas City: Kansas City Star Books, 2002.

Gabler, Neal. *Walt Disney: The Triumph of the American Imagination.* New York: Knopf, 2006.

Green, Amy Boothe and Green, Howard E. *Remembering Walt: Favorite Memories of Walt Disney.* New York: Hyperion, 1999.

Smith, Dave. *Disney: The First 100 Years*. New York: Hyperion, 1999.

Susanin, Timothy S. and Miller, Diane Disney. *Walt Before Mickey: Disney's Early Years, 1919–1928*. Jackson, MS: University Press of Mississippi, 2011.

Thomas, Bob. *Walt Disney: An American Original*. New York: Disney Editions, 1994.

Walt Disney Archives. *History of the Walt Disney Company*.

Walt Disney Archives. *Walt Disney Biography*.

Walt Disney Archives. *Walt's Files, Byline Stories, Folder #3 of Complete Set*.

Walt Disney Archives. *Walt's Files, Questions Answered by Walt*.